CONTENTS

FIGURES

ACRONYMS AND DEFINITIONS

ARP	Address Resolution Protocol
DCOM	Distributed Common Object Model
DHS	U.S. Department of Homeland Security
DMZ	Demilitarized Zone
DNP	Distributed Network Protocol
FTP	File Transfer Protocol
HMI	Human Machine Interface
ICCP	Inter Control Center Communications Protocol
ICS-CERT	Industrial Control Systems Cyber Emergency Response Team
IDS	Intrusion Detection Systems
IP	Internet Protocol
IT	Information Technology
LAN	Local Area Network
MitM	Man-in-the-Middle
NERC	North American Electrical Reliability Corporation
NIST	National Institute of Standards and Technology
NSA	National Security Agency
OLE	Object Linking and Embedding
OPC	OLE for Process Control
OPSEC	Operational Security
PLC	Programmable Logic Controller
RPC	Remote Procedure Call
SCADA	Supervisory Control and Data Acquisition
SIEM	Security Incident Event Management
SQL	Structured Query Language
TCP	Transmission Control Protocol
US-CERT	U.S. Computer Emergency Readiness Team
VoIP	Voice-over Internet Protocol
WARDIALING	Recursive dialing of phone numbers from a modem-enabled PC in an attempt to locate other unadvertised modems resulting in unauthorized access into a computing or Process Control System domain
WARDRIVING	Recursive searching for wireless access points in an attempt to access a communication network resulting in unauthorized access into a computing or control system domain

Recommended Practice: Improving Industrial Control Systems Cybersecurity with Defense-In-Depth Strategies

1. INTRODUCTION

Information infrastructures across many public and private domains share several common attributes regarding information technology (IT) deployments and data communications. This is particularly true in the industrial control systems domain where an increasing number of organizations are using modern networking to enhance productivity and reduce costs by increasing the integration of external, business, and control system networks. However, these integration strategies often lead to vulnerabilities that greatly reduce the cybersecurity posture of an organization and can expose mission-critical industrial control systems to cyber threats.

This document provides guidance for developing "defense-in-depth" strategies for organizations that use control system networks while maintaining multitier information architectures.

1.1 Background

The critical infrastructure systems that support major industries, such as manufacturing, transportation, and energy, are highly dependent on information systems for their command and control. While a high dependence on legacy industrial control systems still exists, critical infrastructure systems are migrating to new communication technologies. As a result, common communications protocols and open architecture standards are replacing the diverse and disparate proprietary mechanics of industrial control systems. This replacement can have both positive and negative impacts.

On the positive side, the migration empowers asset owners to access new and more efficient methods of communication as well as more robust data, quicker time to market, and interoperability. On the negative side, empowering control system users with contemporary computing capabilities can introduce new risks. Cyber-related vulnerabilities and risks are being created that did not exist when industrial control systems were isolated. A number of instances have illustrated the interdependence[1] of industrial control systems, such as those in the power sector, including the 2003 North American blackout. In order to effectively understand an industrial control system security posture, a risk model is needed that more effectively maps to these complex systems. Control systems can affect things in the physical world, and as a result, the definition of risk as it applies to an industrial control system will need to include consideration for consequences. More specifically, risk can be better defined as a function of vulnerabilities multiplied by threats and consequences.

New protocols and communication standards that provide increased interoperability in the industrial control systems community are, in many cases, the same technologies that have been exploited and compromised on the Internet and corporate networking domains. The migration from older legacy-type architectures to modern operating systems and platforms can force industrial control systems to inherit many cybersecurity vulnerabilities, with some of these vulnerabilities having countermeasures that often cannot be deployed in automation systems.

Figure 1 illustrates the traditional separation of corporate architectures and control domains. This architecture provided means for data sharing, data acquisition, peer-to-peer data exchange, and other business operations. However, the security of any given system was based on the fact that few, if any, understood the intricate architecture or the operational mechanics of the resources on the controls system local area network (LAN). This "security by obscurity" generally works well for environments that have no external communication connections, thus allowing an organization to focus on physical security.

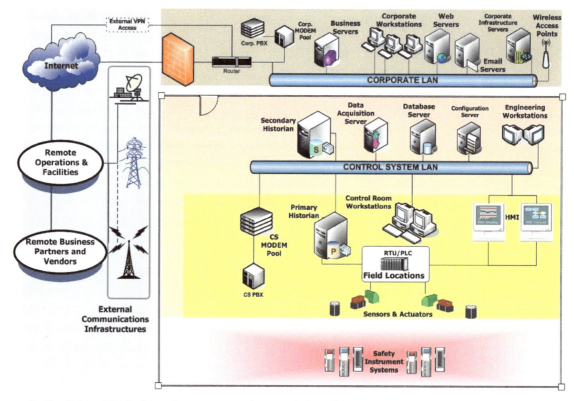

Figure 1. Traditional isolation of corporate and control domains.

1.2 Overview of Contemporary Industrial Control System Architectures

The increasing convergence of once-isolated industrial control systems has helped organizations simplify and manage their complex environments. In connecting these networks and introducing IT components into the industrial control system domain, security problems arise because of:

- Increasing dependency on automation and industrial control systems

- Insecure connectivity to external networks

- Usage of technologies with known vulnerabilities, creating previously unseen cyber risk in the control domain

- Lack of a qualified cybersecurity business case for industrial control system environments

- Some control system technologies have limited security and are often only enabled if the administrator is aware of the capability (or the security does not impede the process)

- Many popular control system communications protocols are absent of basic security functionality (i.e., authentication, authorization)

- Considerable amount of open source information that is available regarding industrial control systems, their operations, and security vulnerabilities.

Control systems operational security has historically been defined by industry as the level of reliability of the system to operate safely and efficiently. The total isolation from the external (and untrusted) network allowed the organization to reduce the overall level of communications security to those threats associated with personnel having physical access to a facility or a plant floor. Thus most data communications in the information infrastructure required limited authorization or security oversight.

Operational commands, instructions, and data acquisition occurred in a closed environment where all communications were trusted. In general, if a command or instruction was sent via the network, it was anticipated to arrive and perform the authorized function because only authorized operators had access to the system.

This is a very different approach when looking to provide effective network and IT cybersecurity. Merging a modern IT architecture with an isolated network that may not have any real cybersecurity countermeasures is challenging. Although simple connectivity using routers and switching is the most obvious means to provide interconnectivity, unauthorized access by an individual could result in unlimited access to the systems. Figure 2 shows an integrated architecture that has connections from external sources such as the corporate LAN, peer sites, vendor sites, and the Internet.

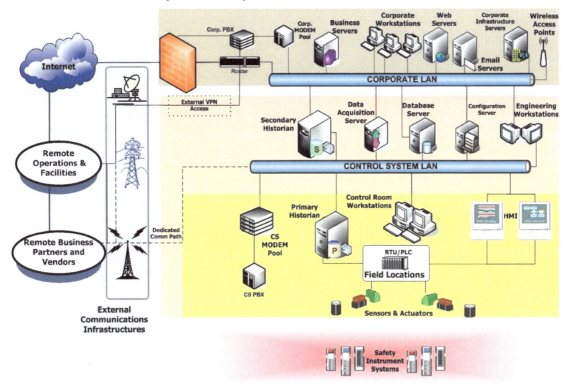

Figure 2. Integrated networks.

From Figure 2, integrated architectures, if compromised, clearly could provide an attacker with various avenues for accessing critical systems, either on the corporate LAN, the control LAN, or even the communications LAN. The very nature of such architectures demands the exchange of data from disparate information sources, of which an attacker could take advantage.

2. SECURITY CHALLENGES WITHIN INDUSTRIAL CONTROL SYSTEMS

Within modern Transmission Control Protocol/Internet Protocol (TCP/IP)-based computing environments, such as the corporate infrastructure for managing the business that drives operations in a control system, technology-related vulnerabilities need to be addressed. Historically, these issues have been the responsibility of the corporate IT security organization, usually governed by security policies and operating plans that protect vital information assets. The main concern as industrial control systems become part of larger conjoined architectures is providing security procedures that cover the control systems domain as well. Contemporary network-based communications have security issues that must be addressed in the control systems domain, because unique vendor-specific protocols and inherent legacy system security may not be adequate to protect mission-critical systems against modern cyber attacks.

Examples of vulnerabilities in open system architectures that could migrate to control system domains include susceptibility to malicious software (including viruses, worms, etc.), escalation of privileges through code manipulation, network reconnaissance and data gathering, covert traffic analysis, and unauthorized intrusions into networks either through or around perimeter defenses. With some of the more modern systems, vulnerabilities also include hostile mobile code such as malicious active content involving JavaScript, applets, VBScript, and Active-X. With a successful intrusion into industrial control system networks come new issue such as reverse engineering of control system protocols, attacks on operator consoles, and unauthorized access into trusted peer networks and remote facilities. To fully translate information security and information assurance into the control systems realm, one must understand the key differences between traditional IT architectures and industrial control systems technology.

From a mitigation perspective, simply deploying IT security technologies into a control system may not be a viable solution. Although modern industrial control systems often use the same underlying protocols that are used in IT and business networks, the very nature of control systems functionality (combined with operational and availability requirements) may make even proven security technologies inappropriate. Some sectors, such as energy, transportation, and chemical, have time sensitive requirements, so the latency and "throughput" issues associated with security strategies may introduce unacceptable delays and degrade or prevent acceptable system performance.

Several key differences exist between traditional IT environments and control system environments insofar as security is concerned. Figure 3 shows some of the more prominent cybersecurity elements that are common to an organization's security function. Figure 3 also suggests how using these elements in either an IT domain or an industrial control systems domain could be leveraged, and how they are addressed in IT domains as opposed to architectures that run industrial control systems.[2]

4

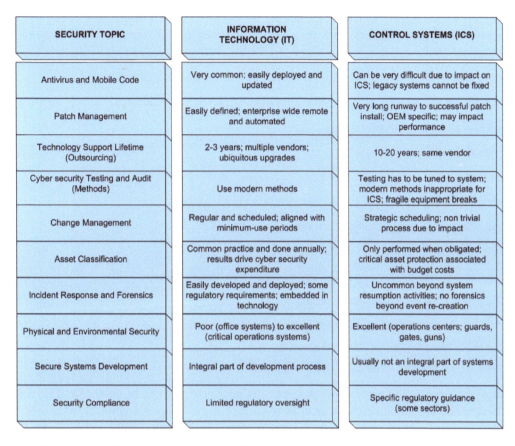

SECURITY TOPIC	INFORMATION TECHNOLOGY (IT)	CONTROL SYSTEMS (ICS)
Antivirus and Mobile Code	Very common; easily deployed and updated	Can be very difficult due to impact on ICS; legacy systems cannot be fixed
Patch Management	Easily defined; enterprise wide remote and automated	Very long runway to successful patch install; OEM specific; may impact performance
Technology Support Lifetime (Outsourcing)	2-3 years; multiple vendors; ubiquitous upgrades	10-20 years; same vendor
Cyber security Testing and Audit (Methods)	Use modern methods	Testing has to be tuned to system; modern methods inappropriate for ICS; fragile equipment breaks
Change Management	Regular and scheduled; aligned with minimum-use periods	Strategic scheduling; non trivial process due to impact
Asset Classification	Common practice and done annually; results drive cyber security expenditure	Only performed when obligated; critical asset protection associated with budget costs
Incident Response and Forensics	Easily developed and deployed; some regulatory requirements; embedded in technology	Uncommon beyond system resumption activities; no forensics beyond event re-creation
Physical and Environmental Security	Poor (office systems) to excellent (critical operations systems)	Excellent (operations centers; guards, gates, guns)
Secure Systems Development	Integral part of development process	Usually not an integral part of systems development
Security Compliance	Limited regulatory oversight	Specific regulatory guidance (some sectors)

Figure 3.Security focus in IT vs. industrial control systems.

2.1   Security Profiles and Attack Methodologies

Typically, a modern information network will prioritize the normal security objectives in the following manner[a]:

Confidentiality	HIGH IMPORTANCE
Integrity	HIGH IMPORTANCE
Availability	LOWER IMPORTANCE

However, because of the need for high availability and the operational requirements of industrial control systems, the security objectives for most control entities are reversed:

Availability	VERY HIGH IMPORTANCE
Integrity	MEDIUM IMPORTANCE
Confidentiality	LOW IMPORTANCE

a. Generally speaking, criticality of Confidentiality, Integrity, and Availability is determined by the business function, and in many cases order of importance can vary among sectors. However, those systems supporting essential critical infrastructures involving quality of life and human safety (and ones that use control systems) tend to require perpetual availability and high integrity of data. These requirements can overshadow the need to protect the data from unauthorized viewing, unless such breach impacts other critical attributes.

Control networks are evolving from stand-alone domains to interconnected networks that coexist with corporate IT environments, thus introducing security threats and vulnerabilities. Critical cybersecurity issues that need to be addressed in the industrial control systems domain are many, but some of the more pressing issues include:

- Backdoors and "holes" (either intentional or not) in the network perimeter

- Devices with little or no security features (modems, legacy control devices, etc.)

- Vulnerabilities in common protocols

- Attacks on field devices

- Database attacks

- Communications hijacking and man-in-the-middle (MitM) attacks

- Improper or nonexistent patching of software and firmware

- Insecure coding techniques

- Improper cybersecurity procedures for internal and external personnel

- Lack of control systems specific mitigation technologies.

Understanding vulnerabilities and the associated attack vectors to exploit them is essential to building effective security mitigation strategies.

2.1.1   Network Perimeter Security Flaws[3]

As in common networking environments, control system domains can be subject to a myriad of vulnerabilities and holes that can provide an attacker a "backdoor" to gain unauthorized access. Often, backdoors are simple shortcomings in the architecture perimeter, or embedded capabilities that are forgotten, unnoticed, or simply disregarded. Adversaries (threats) often do not require physical access to a domain to gain access to it and will usually leverage any discovered access functionality. Modern networks, especially those in the control systems arena, often have inherent capabilities that are deployed without sufficient security analysis and can provide access to attackers once they are discovered. These backdoors can be accidentally created in various places on the network, but it is the network perimeter that is of greatest concern.

When looking at network perimeter components, the modern IT architecture will have technologies to provide for robust remote access. These technologies often include firewalls, public facing services, and wireless access. Each technology will allow enhanced communications in and amongst affiliated networks and will often be a subsystem of a much larger and more complex information infrastructure. However, each of these components can (and often do) have associated security vulnerabilities that an attacker will try to detect and leverage. Interconnected networks are particularity attractive to the attacker, because a single point of compromise may provide extended access due to pre-existing trust established among interconnected resources.

The network perimeter has also been extended through the common use of wireless communications, especially for very remote sites. The extended perimeter has opened new holes for attack vectors because unsecured wireless access is a recurring element in many organizations. Such deployments are common due to the ease-of-use of wireless communications as well as a low level of understanding regarding security implications of wireless deployments. Moreover, in the plant floor environment, wireless technology is easier to deploy than traditional wired infrastructures, which can require drilling through walls and laying cable. Vendors have embraced the usefulness of wireless and radio-based communications, and many have full suites of wireless-based solutions.

Common security issues with wireless communications often include the residual effects of default installations. Attackers, once having discovered wireless communications points, can leverage the inherent functionality of wireless networks to their advantage and take advantage of Service Set Identifier (SSID) broadcasting, limited access controls, lack of encryption, and limited network segmentation. When considering the historical characteristics of control system networks, especially those that impact security because of the presence of plaintext traffic and inherent trust relationships, unauthorized access (via a wireless access point) into the control domain can provide an attacker with a very effective backdoor, often bypassing security perimeters.

Some of the more recent research has discovered some significant service-based vulnerabilities in the 802.15.4 protocol, weaknesses that could lead to jamming and denial of service. Some after-market modifications to protocol implementations, such as those done to create larger address spaces, can reduce security safeguards to meet interoperability requirements.

Although much of the complexity in maintaining secure systems can be avoided by proper patch management programs, a major problem for control system units is when both geography and accessibility to devices are a concern. Disparate control system elements that can be accessed via remote communications require special consideration. Often, if systems are based on commercial operating systems, the attacks can be via denial of service, escalated privilege exploits, or clandestine tools such as a Trojan horse or logic bomb.

Modern computing technology has allowed for control system operations to be performed from a distance, and with that the security perimeter has been relocated to the point where the remote access originates. This creates new demands for security administrators in trying to manage these connections while preventing the compromise of vital command and control functions. Compromising a computing resource that has administrative access to a control system is, in many cases, the same as compromising the operator console itself. This concern relates to the interception, modification, and reinjection of control data into a network, or the possibility of an attacker escalating privileges within the control domain to execute engineering level instructions across the control signal communications loop.

Information collected from the control systems has always been used by control system owners as a key component in business decision-making, such as in calculating load and demand projections. To support customer service, organizations in many sectors provide data to customers, providers, and affiliates through publicly accessible servers. The data on these servers are usually sourced from the business domain (after it is collected from the control or field operations domain) as well as collected from the public domain.

This interconnected capability, as effective as it is, is also a vector for attackers to gain access into the protected business networks and perhaps the industrial control system networks. Attackers can often collect important information from these public servers, including data regarding operations, customers, and file transfers. Moreover, if the servers are compromised, the attackers can escalate their privileges and pivot their attack to compromise back-end business networks or even the control networks. A simple example of this is in the area of Advanced Metering Infrastructure, where energy usage data from customers is aggregated, processed, presented, and used for billing. Because Advanced Metering Infrastructure is a two-way operation, such integrated command and control can also lead to vulnerabilities that, if exploited, could impede utility operations.

Organizations with firewalls to separate pubic servers from internal networks often find it hard to defend against these types of attacks. To allow robust information to be provided via external services, such as a web or FTP server, communication must be made from the web server to the internal databases or historians, and this connection is made via the firewall. If deployed without effective security countermeasures, the trust relationship between the firewall and the web server allows data to flow from the external side to the internal domain. If these data are unauthorized and are the product of an attack that has compromised the trusted web server, the attacker has a channel to access internal services on the business (or industrial control systems) LAN.

In general, a delicate balance exists between business functionality and security. This balance has to be evaluated properly and revisited often. The deployment of modern technology to increase productivity and access requires special attention to prevent backdoors into the business or control system networks.

2.1.2   Attacks Using Common Protocols, i.e., OPC/DCOM Attacks[4]

The impact of modern operating systems on industrial control systems has been significant. Over the last several years, more and more organizations have started to use underlying services in these environments, some of them being the Object Link and Embedding (OLE), Distributed Component Object Model (DCOM), and Remote Procedure Call (RPC). OLE for Process Control (OPC) is a real-time data communications standard based in these services. Many installations are moving away from the Microsoft-based OPC model. However, OPC is still commonly used for efficient connectivity with diverse industrial control systems equipment. Also, OPC is widely deployed on mission critical components of a control systems environment such as, human machine interface (HMI) workstations, historians, and many Enterprise Resource Planning systems highlighting the continued dependency on OPC. A recent study showed that many industrial control systems and their processes would have permanent historical data and production time loss if an OPC service was to become unavailable[5]

OPC standards and application programming interfaces that are common in control system environments are OPC Data Access 3.0, OPC Alarms, OPC Data Exchange, and OPC Data-XML. All OPC standards and application programming interfaces are widely supported and used in Windows XP and Windows Server additions. A wide variety of security implications and vulnerabilities have been identified with OPC services and standards. Vulnerabilities range from simple system enumeration and password vulnerabilities to more complex remote registry tampering and buffer overflow flaws. These vulnerabilities expose many industrial control systems with critical risks such as the installation of undetected malware, denial-of-service attacks, escalated privileges on a host, and/or the accidental shutdown of industrial control systems because of an overload flaw.

Even though many of these vulnerabilities have solutions and available workarounds, the deployment of these mitigations in industrial control system architectures have not always resulted in success. For example, Windows XP Service Pack 2 by default can change settings on the host machine, making DCOM applications that connect to a remote server unavailable. To ensure compatibility, large scale in-house testing of DCOM and OPC-dependent applications was needed but not completed. Many organizations were impacted by these default settings and have yet to upgrade or change their applications and have skipped upgrading to Service Pack 2. Furthermore, Microsoft has updated their recommended practice for distributed programming, moving toward a service-oriented architecture based on the .NET framework and away from DCOM. The lack of support in the future for DCOM and OPC standards, along with the long life cycles of industrial control systems, could see many organizations still deploying OPC and DCOM without any vendor support. Historically, many popular operating systems have a history of being plagued with security vulnerabilities, and when combined with future state deployments that are devoid of vendor support, security problems can manifest in a myriad of ways.

2.1.3   Attack into Control Systems via Field Devices

Industrial control systems architectures usually have a capability for remote access to terminal end points and telemetry devices. In some cases, the field equipment itself has the capability to be accessed a number of ways, including by telephonic or dedicated means. To provide for the collection of operational and maintenance data, some modern equipment has embedded file servers and web servers to facilitate robust communications. Engineers and administrators often have a secondary means of communicating with these field devices using this access capability in addition to other dedicated communications channels.

For example, many control system architectures are designed to have remote connections using either publicly accessible telephone networks or dedicated lines for modem access. When left unsecured, an attacker can connect remotely with little effort, and the remote connection may be difficult to detect (assuming little monitoring or logging). Secured modems that have user identities and passwords are still susceptible to attacks through war dialing and brute-force cracking. As is often the case, there are often no automated account lockouts based on repeated unsuccessful login attempts.[6] This once considered obsolete reconnaissance method is seeing a rapid resurgence due to Voice-over Internet Protocol (VoIP) and the common knowledge of many critical systems still using dialup for remote control.[b]

In addition, field devices are part of an internal and trusted domain, and thus access into these devices can provide an attacker with a vector into the control systems architecture. By gaining access into a field device, the attacker can become part of the sensor network and tunnel back into the control systems network. Recognizing that field devices are an extension of the control domain, attackers can add these field devices to their list of viable targets to be investigated during reconnaissance and scanning phases of the attack. Although such attacks typically are not possible across serial connections, the security related to the convergence of modern networking protocols and traditional control protocols in remote devices requires attention.

If a device is compromised, and the attacker can leverage control over the device and cause unauthorized actions, the attacker can begin to execute a number of procedures, including scanning back into the internal control network, altering the data that will be sent to the control master, or changing the behavior of the device itself. If the attacker decides to scan back into the control network, which would leverage the trust between resources, it may be possible to do so by using the actual communications protocols for the entire control systems domain. This is of particular advantage to the attacker because the connections are not monitored for malicious or suspect traffic.[c]

2.1.4   Database and SQL Data Injection Attacks[7]

Database applications have become core application components of industrial control systems and their associated record keeping utilities. Traditional security models attempt to secure systems by isolating core control system components and concentrating security efforts against threats specific to those computers or software components. Database security within industrial control systems follows these models by using generally independent systems that rely on one another for proper functionality. The high level of reliance between the two systems creates an expanded threat surface.

Databases used by industrial control systems are often connected to databases or computers with web-enabled applications located on the business network. Virtually every data-driven application has transitioned to some form of database. Most use Structured Query Language (SQL), and many will have web interfaces that may be vulnerable to typical web attacks like XSS or SQL injection.

The information contained in databases makes them high-value targets for any attacker. When control system databases are connected to business or financial databases or to computers with applications used to access the data, attackers can exploit the communications channel between the two networks and bypass the security mechanisms used to protect the control systems environment.

---

b. Published tools have created software leveraging VoIP systems that can wardial up to a thousand numbers hourly.

c. Some intrusion detection systems (IDS) can be updated with industrial control systems signatures to help defend control domains. Usually, these systems are signature-based and will trigger on seeing recognized malicious traffic. In lieu of viable signature, IDS can be deployed to trigger on nonspecific traffic, or upon seeing traffic that is not expected or unusual. See below for the discussion on IDS.

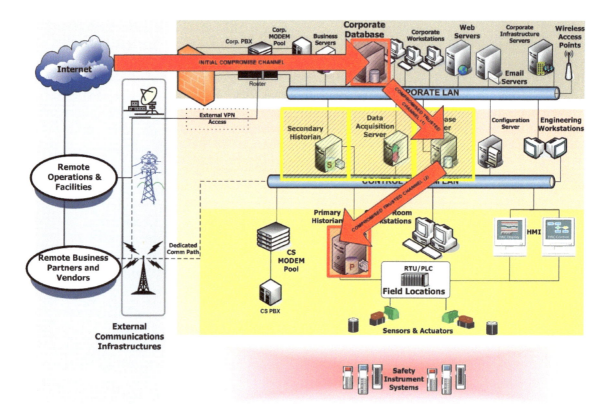

Figure 4. Attacking via databases.

Figure 4 shows an example of the open connectivity between databases. This example illustrates a communication path between the servers that an attacker would be able to leverage to gain access to the control network. Injection into a database with valuable data can have far-reaching effects, especially in a control systems environment where data accuracy and integrity are critical for both business and operational decision-making. The cascading effect of corrupted database content can impact data acquisition servers, historians, and even the operator HMI console. Industrial control systems are more adversely affected by SQL injection than are many general IT databases because they are so reliant on data availability and integrity. Moreover, compromise of key trusted assets, such as a database, creates additional resources the attacker can use for both reconnaissance and code execution.

Given the reliance of industrial control systems on the storage, accuracy, and accessibility of command and control data, as well as the prevalence of SQL databases on these types of networks, standard SQL injection techniques against control system components pose a major threat to control systems security.

2.1.5   Man-in-the-Middle Attacks[8]

Control system environments have traditionally been (or been intended to be) protected from nonauthorized persons by air gapping. In these networks, data that flow between servers, resources, and devices are often less secured. Three security issues that arise from assumed trust are (1) the ability for an attacker to reroute data that are in transit on a network, (2) the ability to capture and analyze critical traffic that is in plaintext format, and (3) the ability to reverse engineer control protocols and gain command over control communications. By combining all these, an attacker could assume exceptionally high control over the data flowing in a network, and ultimately direct both real and "spoofed" traffic to network resources in support of the desired outcome. To do this, a Man-in-the-Middle, or MITM, attack is executed.

Management of addresses in a network, be it a control systems or a business LAN, is critical to effective operations. Address Resolution Protocol (ARP) helps maintain routing by helping map network addresses to physical machine addresses. Using ARP tables in each of the network devices ensures that computers and other devices know how to route their traffic when requesting communication. Manipulation (or poisoning) of the ARP tables is a key goal of the attacker, because poisoning the ARP tables can force all network traffic (including control traffic) to be routed through the computer the attacker has compromised. In this manner, all resources on the network will have to "talk" to the attacker without knowing they are communicating with the attacker. Moreover, the attacker can see, capture, replay, and inject data into the network and have it interpreted as if it were authorized and coming from a trusted source.

Assuming an attacker has gained access onto the controls systems network, perhaps using any of the aforementioned attacks, he will use network reconnaissance to determine resources that are available on that network. As the attack is on the control domain, plaintext traffic can be captured (sniffed) and taken offline for analysis and review. This allows the attacker to review and re-engineer packet and payload content, modify the instruction set to accommodate the goal of the attack, and reinject the new (and perhaps malicious) packet into the network. Control traffic, regardless of its unique nature, is not very complex insofar as the nomenclature used for instruction in data payloads. The data contained in the packets are used to control the action of the field devices and to provide input as to what is seen by the operator at the HMI workstation.

By using ARP poisoning and collecting traffic, the attacker can establish and maintain control over the communications in the network. If the attacker needs to acquire and analyze unique control system protocols, control data can be seen, captured, and manipulated. The time required to reverse engineer key control data, and manipulate that data for nefarious purposes can vary depending on the skill of the attacker and the complexity of the data. However, by taking the data offline, the attacker is now able to work at a tempo that is most appropriate for him or her.

In any environment, MitM attacks are exceptionally dangerous. However, in the industrial control system networks this mode of attack becomes even more critical. A MitM attack can exploit common vulnerabilities in industrial control systems, such as weak authentication protocols or poor integrity checking in firmware.[9] Exploiting vulnerabilities that are common to control systems creates a larger attack surface, which in turn could increase the likeliness of a successful attack. Furthermore, by assuming control of a key information resource and performing a MitM attack, an unauthorized intruder can attack the system by:

- Stopping operations

- Capturing, modifying, and replaying control data

- Injecting inaccurate data to falsify information in key databases, timing clocks, and historians

- Replaying normal operational data to the operator HMI while executing a malicious attack on the field device (while preventing the HMI from issuing alarms).

2.1.6   Improper or Nonexistent OS and Application Patching

As stated previously, the technology life cycle of typical industrial control systems is very long and can range anywhere between 10 and 20 years. Because of this long technology life cycle, many industrial control systems are running firmware and operating systems with published vulnerabilities. This security issue is exacerbated by a common over-reliance on isolating industrial control systems and not supporting a proper patch management operational procedure. A typical IT operational security program will have a security program that not only monitors for vulnerabilities that are published by vendor or through a third party but will also set up a consistent process to review and install security patches. A vast majority of control networks use the same operating systems that can be found in an IT department. The same types of OS level vulnerabilities will make a control system open for an attack. Some progressive control system environments may have a patch management procedure. But, this procedure is typically a manual process and can take a very long time to patch a system because of the distances that may be between sites, or a lack of resources with the proper training.

Most control system operations are very cautious regarding patching systems because deploying a security patch can involve a significant amount of testing while at the same time risking the availability (and safety) of the system. A security testing process will be difficult to execute if proper testing resources, such as a redundant lab, staging area, or test facility, are lacking. Also, some patches will break a current process or software implementation causing some control system operations to skip the patch process altogether and assume the risk.

In addition, the patching problem is the issue of updating firmware in a timely manner. Firmware updates can include security level patches that if not installed on the host device's memory will leave the device vulnerable to the security issue the patch was intended to resolve. Although firmware updates are usually not as frequent as software or OS level patches, firmware updates can be very time consuming.

Some modern day hardware devices can be updated remotely and automatically. However in many cases, a legacy industrial control system's hardware will need to be physically connected to or, in a worse-case scenario, will need to be fully replaced in order to gain the benefits of the new firmware.

2.1.7   Insecure Coding Techniques

Because of the complexity and "for purpose" requirements, many control system implementations have insecure code inherent in them. Some industrial control systems have very old programming code that was either custom built or is no longer supported by a vendor. The program code can suffer from insecurities for multiple reasons. For example, many control environments have been built by personnel with little or no security training from a programming perspective. Custom applications have not gone through a proper cycle of security testing, and many lack any sort of documentation or proper comments within the code. Common programming security flaws, such as buffer overflows or inconsistent input validation, will make unsupported vendor code or custom applications vulnerable to attacks such as those of the denial-of-service type.

Another security issue with common control systems programming is a lack of any authentication or encryption within the application. Many examples can be found of code that is not obfuscated and is in clear text making an attack easier to execute. Encryption of code might not be available for legacy applications, and custom written code might be viewed as too slow if encrypted. Although many applications (if attacked) might not be viewed as a risk, the same application when compromised can be used as an attack vector to another more critical system. Compromising systems with little or no authentication mechanisms can make the success of an attack more likely and will make responding to an incident more difficult because the compromised system may have to be taken offline for repair.

Custom applications and legacy code are not the only vectors of insecure programming attacks. Many vendors of the base software used to run the systems have had vulnerable code exposed and publicized. Sometimes, the vendor of the software may not be in a position to support a robust security audit program in their software development cycle. In recent years, many larger vendors have released patches to their software but the time between vulnerability disclosure and released patched software is usually much longer than a typical IT vendor.

2.1.8   Improper Cybersecurity Procedures

With the integration of networks and the growing complexity of operating a large control system, the personnel that have access to the control networks have grown. Along with the growth of external access, the linking of remote business partners and peer sites has increased. Another attack path is the wide use of modems within an industrial control system environment. Often modems are improperly managed from a security perspective as they are left always on and have not set any type of authentication. Even with a robust procedure for access into a control system through a remote capability, many control system devices have poor logging capabilities and have not been properly turned on for auditing purposes.

Standards for these control system securities have started to emerge. NERC-CIP 002-009 is now mandated for the electrical sector and many electrical organizations have started to comply. Smaller electrical operations may find compliance too complicated and costly and may start late on their compliance efforts. Other standards, such as NIST SP 800-53 (with its revisions) support securing industrial control systems, but many organizations outside of the electrical sector might avoid compliance while waiting for a sector-specific mandate from a governing body.

2.1.9   Lack of Control Systems Specific Security Technologies

Administrators of typical IT environments have a wide variety of vendors to choose from to help implement security and mitigate risks. An IT security operation can choose from multiple large vendors with a wide variety of security products or go with a heterogeneous security posture taking support from multiple vendors. For a control systems environment, the choice for security technologies is specific to the unique needs of the environment. Some common IT vendor offerings can be modified or customized for industrial control systems, but the process can be very complex, very costly, and take a strong commitment from the IT vendor that might not have the expertise to assist in a timely manner. Furthermore, the use of legacy systems that were not built with a robust security features set can make for a wider attack surface.

3.   ISOLATING AND PROTECTING ASSETS: DEFENSE-IN-DEPTH STRATEGIES

As industrial control systems grow in complexity and are connected to business and external networks, the number of security issues and the associated risks with those issues grow as well. The wide variety of attack vectors that target multiple resources on control systems can give rise to attacks that can be executed asynchronously, over a long period of time and could target multiple weaknesses and vulnerabilities of a control systems environment. A single countermeasure cannot be depended on to mitigate all security issues. In order to effectively protect industrial control systems from cyber attacks, multiple countermeasures are needed that will disseminate risk over an aggregate of security mitigation techniques.

The strategy of implementing multiple layers of defense to combat multiple security issues is commonly referred to as defense-in-depth. Figure 5 illustrates the use of multiple layers of defense in order to protect against vulnerabilities, using the case of a Buffer Overflow as a known vulnerability.[d] The strategy is based on using appropriate security countermeasures across operational, network, and host functionality, and having the aggregate of all security activities provide complete protection over the entire architecture.

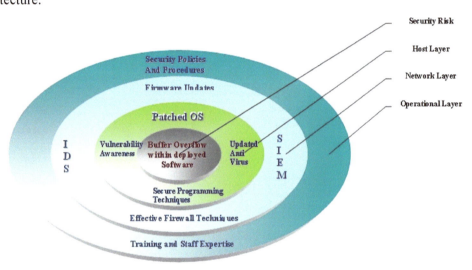

Figure 5. Layered defense for protection against vulnerabilities (i.e., Buffer Overflow).

3.1   Defense-In-Depth Strategic Framework

Cybersecurity, from a defense-in-depth perspective, is not just about deploying specific technologies to counter certain risks. An effective security program for an organization will depend on its adherence and willingness to accept security as a constant *constraint* on all cyber activities. Implementing an effective defense-in-depth strategy will require taking a holistic approach and leveraging all of an organization's resources in order to provide effective layers of protection. Leveraging work done by National Security Agency (NSA),[10] Figure 6 displays an overview on the key elements of a defense-in-depth strategic framework.

---

d. IDS – Intrusion Detection System(s), SIEM – Security Incident and Event Management

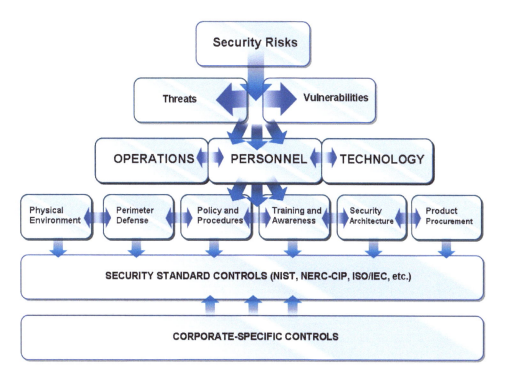

Figure 6. Strategic framework for cyber defense-in-depth.

The basic tenets of this framework are as follows:

1. Know the security risks that an organization faces

2. Quantify and qualify risks

3. Use key resources to mitigate security risks

4. Define each resource's core competency and identify any overlapping areas

5. Abide by existing or emerging security standards for specific controls

6. Create and customize specific controls that are unique to an organization.

An organization implementing a defense-in-depth strategy will need to start at understanding its current risk. Risk for industrial control systems is best understood by knowing the threats and vulnerabilities that face an organization. In order to understand risk, an organization should undergo a rigorous risk assessment that covers all aspects of the organization. Risk assessments are a key cornerstone in defining, understanding, and planning remediation efforts against specific threats and vulnerabilities. Valuable risk assessments are constantly updated on timely intervals, supported by all areas and levels of the organization, including C-level executives.

In order to create a culture for protecting industrial control systems, a cross functional team needs to be assembled. The team should include at least one executive level manager for leadership and guidance, security and operations management at the corporate level, and full participation from control system engineers and managers. The team will need to be trained on the key aspects of industrial control systems cybersecurity and be fully aware of the present security challenges and risks that the organization needs to address in regard to its own industrial control systems infrastructure.

The team will be responsible for developing policies and procedures that will increase the security capability and protection of industrial control systems. Sound guidance for an industrial control system will need to address all the operational requirements first. This will ensure new security policies do not negatively affect the availability of the industrial control systems. Once the operational requirements are clearly understood, a full operational security program (OPSEC) can be built.[11] The OPSEC program should include clear boundaries for roles and responsibilities and include elements that describe the day-to-day management operations for physical security, access control, and safeguarding a strong perimeter defense.

In support of the personnel and OPSEC program, technology can now be put into place that addresses specific needs of the organization's industrial control systems. Proper defense-in-depth technological deployment starts with a robust technology assessment plan, a procurement process that specifically requires security capabilities before purchase,[12] and an implementation plan that enforces security throughout the system life cycle. Technology in an industrial control system should be viewed as part of a larger security architecture that recognizes key areas of interconnectivity and architectural security capabilities.

3.1.1   Architectural Zones

In order to create a layered defense, a clear understanding is essential of how all the technology fits together and where all the interconnectivity resides. Dividing common control systems architecture into zones can assist organizations in creating clear boundaries in order to effectively apply multiple layers of defense. Vital to creating architectural zones involves understanding how network segmentation can be achieved. Methodologies for segmenting networks within and around control system environments can leverage best practices and can include (but not necessarily be limited to):

1. Firewalls (single, multi-homed, dual, cascading)

2. Routers with Access Control Lists (ACLs)

3. Configured switches

4. Static routes and routing tables

5. Dedicated communications media.

Expanding on the Purdue Model for Control Hierarchy,[13] the following zones segment information architecture into five basic functions:

1. <u>External Zone</u> is the area of connectivity to the Internet, peer locations, and backup or remote offsite facilities. This is not a demilitarized zone (DMZ) but is the point of connectivity that is usually considered untrusted. For industrial control systems, the external zone has the least amount of priority and the highest variety of risks.

2. <u>Corporate Zone</u> is the area of connectivity for corporate communications. E-mail servers, DNS servers, and IT business system infrastructure components are typical resources in this zone. A wide variety of risks exist in this zone because of the amount of systems and connectivity to the External Zone. However, because of the maturity of the security posture and redundancy of systems, the Corporate Zone's precedence can be considered to be at a lower priority than other zones, but much higher than the External Zone.

3. <u>Manufacturing/Data Zone</u> is the area of connectivity where a vast majority of monitoring and control takes place. It is a critical area for continuity and management of a control network. Operational support and engineering management devices are located in this zone along side data acquisition servers and historians. The Manufacturing Zone is central in the operation of both the end devices and the business requirements of the Corporate Zone, and the priority of this area is considered to be high. Risks are associated with direct connectivity to the External Zone and the Corporate Zone.

4. <u>Control/Cell Zone</u> is the area of connectivity to devices such as Programmable Logic Controllers (PLCs), HMIs, and basic input/output devices such as actuators and sensors. The priority of this zone

is very high as this is the area where the functions of the devices affect the physical end devices. In a modern control network, these devices will have support for TCP/IP and other common protocols.

5. <u>Safety Zone</u> usually has the highest priority because these devices have the ability to automatically control the safety level of an end device (such as Safety Instrument Systems). Typically, the risk is lower in this zone as these devices are only connected to the end devices but recently many of these devices have started to offer functionality for TCP/IP connectivity for the purposes of remote monitoring and redundancy support.

Figure 7 illustrates a common modern architecture that contains all these zones.

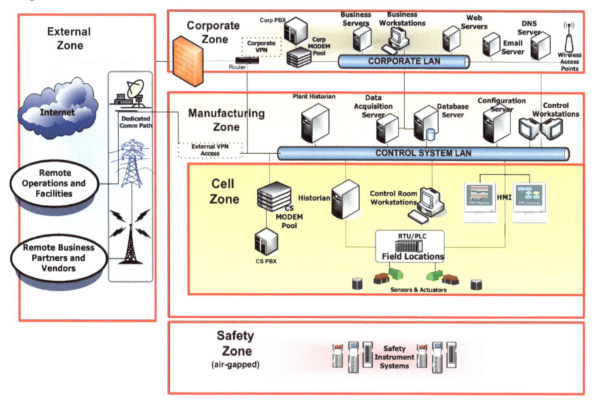

Figure 7. Common architecture zones.

Each of these zones requires a unique security focus. A "peel-the-onion" analysis shows that an attacker trying to affect a critical infrastructure system would most likely be after the core control domain.[e] Manipulation of the industrial control systems information resources can be devastating if this critical zone is compromised. In many sectors, the malicious attack on the control systems will have real-world, physical results.

In this document, and in the suggested supporting documentation provided by U.S. Department of Homeland Security (DHS) through U.S. Computer Emergency Readiness Team (US-CERT), numerous categories of attacks and outcomes have been discussed. In each of those scenarios, the intrusion begins at some point outside the control zone, and the attacker pries deeper and deeper into the architecture.

---

e. This, of course, depends on the overall objective of the attacker. In general, complete control over core services and operational capability of the control system has high value.

Thus, defensive strategies that secure each of the core zones can create a defensive strategy with depth, offering the administrators more opportunities for information and resources control as well as introducing cascading countermeasures that will not necessarily impede business functionality.

3.2 Firewalls

Firewalls provide additional levels of defense that support the traditional routers, providing the capability to add much tighter and more complex rules for communication between the different network segments or zones. Of critical importance to industrial control systems is how the firewall is implemented and, to a certain degree, how the core functionality of the firewall impacts the overall business functionality of the environment.

Many types of firewalls are available, and some research is required to ascertain what type of firewall is right for a given control architecture. In addition, as different firewalls can operate in support of different layers within the OSI model, consideration should be given to what controls system applications and connectivity will be crossing boundaries (if any). To understand how firewalls work, it helps to understand how the different layers of a network interact. Network architectures, including control system architectures that leverage the model, are designed around a model composed of seven layers. The OSI model allows networks to combine different protocols and support physical connectivity. Firewalls, which are often points of ingress and egress for a network (zones), will operate at different layers to use different criteria to restrict traffic. This is vital to the successful deployment of firewalls, especially when developing solutions to segregate networks. The lowest layer at which a firewall can work is layer three, and in the OSI model this is the network layer.[f] This is the layer of the model that handles routing, and as such is able to allow a device (such as a firewall) to ascertain if connections are allowed but cannot assess the packet contents for validity.

As such, the firewalls that can provide more analysis and "inspection" of packets operate higher in the layers and into the transport layer. These firewalls can provide a more granular investigation of data and can either permit or deny on payload. Firewalls that work at the application layer can often provide a significant amount of information about user activities and data structures. However, a word of caution — although a firewall operating higher in the stack may appear to be superior in many aspects, that is not always the case.

The concept of security zones, as discussed earlier, provides some insight as to how an organization can determine what risk and consequence is associated with a particular zone. This analysis can be used to select the type of firewall and attributes that are best suited for protecting the assets. In general, four main types of firewalls exist:

6. Packet filter (work at the Network layer)

7. Circuit level gateways (work at the Session layer)

8. Proxy gateways (work at the Application layer)

9. Stateful inspection (work at Network, Session, and Application layers).

3.2.1 Packet Filter Firewalls

These firewalls analyze the packets going into and out of separated networks and either permit or deny passage based on a pre-established set of rules. Packet filtering rules are based on port numbers, protocols, and other defined data that correlate to the type of data request being made. Although usually flexible in assigning rules, this type of firewall is well suited for environments where quick connections

---

f The TCP/IP model has existed for longer than the OSI model and does not align in every layer. From a comparison perspective, the first four layers of TCP/IP are analogous to OSI, and interoperability is commonplace.

are required and rules can be developed based on device addresses. Environments, such as industrial control systems, need this effective security based on unique applications and protocols.

3.2.2   Proxy Gateway Firewalls

These firewalls are critical in hiding the networks they are protecting and are used as primary gateways to proxy the connection initiated by a protected resource. Often called *application-level* gateways, they are similar to circuit-level gateways except that they address the application. They filter at the Application Layer of the Open Systems Interconnectivity model and do not allow any connections for which no proxy is available. These firewalls are good for analyzing data inside the application (POST, GET, etc.) as well as collecting data about user activities (logon, admin, etc.). The firewalls are gateways and require users to direct their connection to the firewall. The firewall also has some impact on network performance because of the nature of the analysis. In industrial control system environments, this type of firewall is well suited to separating the business and control LANs as well as providing protection to a DMZ and other assets that require application-specific defenses.

3.2.3   Host Firewalls

Host firewalls are a software solution that protects ports and services specifically for the device on which it is installed. Some third-party software packages are host-based firewalls, but many modern day operating systems for servers, workstations, laptops, and other devices have host firewalls integrated into them. Host firewalls have the ability to create rule sets that track, allow, or deny incoming and outgoing traffic on the device. Modern day operating systems have preinstalled host firewalls that can be customized to help protect other systems ports and services. These firewalls are integrated into the operating system itself and have customization capabilities that can be very useful in protecting the host. Host-based firewalls can be a very important feature for mobile devices and laptops because they may exit and enter the industrial control systems domain. As well, depending on the age of the operating system on devices like HMIs and engineering workstations, an industrial control system may be able to take advantage of host-based firewalls to add an extra layer of security.

3.2.3.1   *Stateful Inspection Firewalls*

Stateful inspection firewalls include characteristics of all the other types of firewalls. They filter at the network layer, determine the legitimacy of the sessions, and evaluate contents of the packets at the application layer. They tend to use algorithms to process data rather than run proxies. These firewalls execute a considerable amount of inspection of packets that are arriving on the interfaces. These firewalls look at the "state" of the packets and analyze against preobserved activities, thus allowing for a higher level of trust when deciding what is allowed. These firewalls are capable of keeping track of valid sessions and make a good choice for protecting key assets in the control domain. Because many of the vulnerabilities in industrial control systems have their roots in trust that is shared among servers and devices, being able to track and react to valid and invalid sessions is advantageous.

3.2.3.2   *PLC/Field Level Firewalls*

PLC field level firewalls are hardware-based firewalls that plug directly in line with device level traffic on a control systems network. These firewalls attempt to add security features to field devices, such as PLCs, Remote Terminal Units, and Distributed Control Systems, that might not already exist on the device. Field device level firewalls are relatively new to the industrial control systems security domain, but their impact can be significant on protecting devices that may not have inherent security capabilities. They can also provide for intrusion detection and be used as a log source to help with unified threat management.

With a wide variety of capabilities for defensive measures, the deployment of firewalls into an industrial control systems environment is crucial for a robust security program. Furthermore, in support of a defense-in-depth security posture, the strategy to deploy layered firewalls throughout the organization is essential. Adding firewalls at all external connection points, including from the industrial control systems network to the corporate network increases the layers of security at all the network perimeter levels. In addition, an excellent firewall deployment technique is to add a second set of firewalls from a different vendor. The two vendor firewalls will match in rules set and configuration but are deployed at the same areas of the architecture. This can help assist in protecting against firmware security holes that might affect one vendor's firewall but not the other's. This adds another layer of defense that can give the defending network perimeter time to patch the firmware on the vulnerable firewall, thus delaying and then thwarting an attack that intended to exploit that vulnerability.

Unfortunately, this can add some managerial and cost overhead but the added protection can outweigh the effort to put it in place. With that identified, Figure 8 illustrates the deployment of layered firewalls in a multizone architecture. In this diagram, as well as related images illustrating network architecture, the Safety Zone is to be considered "air-gapped" and is not connected to the architecture.[g]

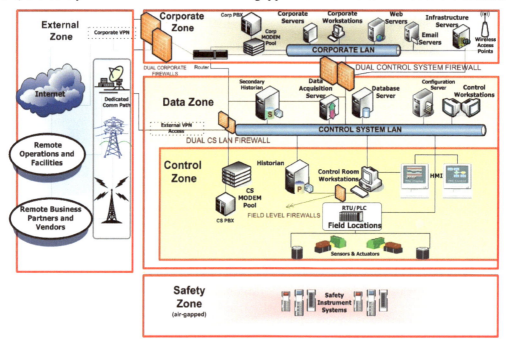

Figure 8. Firewalls protecting architecture zones.

Well-configured firewalls are critical to industrial control systems security. Communications should be restricted to that necessary for system functionality. More importantly, communication paths into and out of specific zones require detailed security risk assessments, and permissions for data exchange along these "conduits" must be developed. As in the development of default rule sets for network equipment, until specific rule sets are established, the communications default should be "denied." Industrial control systems traffic should be monitored, and rules should be developed that allow only necessary access. Any exceptions created in the firewall rule set should be as specific as possible, including host, protocol, and port information.

A common oversight in deploying control system networks is not restricting outbound traffic from the control domain. Firewall rules should consider both directions through the firewall. Most administrators effectively block traffic into the control network, but do not filter traffic out of the network. Outbound

---

g. Safety systems have historically been completely isolated from the control environment, and communications to and from safety systems have been via out-of-band communications. However, some future architectures under consideration have these systems networked together and networked with the control zone.

traffic rules should also be created, and such rules should initially have no exceptions. These rules should be fine-tuned so a rule set that excludes all unnecessary traffic is created. Once the necessary outbound traffic has been determined, a safer configuration can then be created that blocks all traffic with exceptions for necessary communication.

Traditionally, the role of the firewalls in defending networks is straightforward. For example, an attacker targeting an industrial control system needs to obtain information from and send files and commands to the industrial control systems network. To remotely control any exploit code running on an industrial control systems computer, a return connection must be established from the control network. With regard to attacking resources in the industrial control systems domain, exploit code must be small and contain just enough code to get an attacker onto the target computer. Generally, not enough space is available to add logic onto the device for the attacker to get advanced functionality. Therefore, additional instructions are needed from the attacker to continue with the discovery portion of the attack. If outbound filtering is implemented correctly, the attacker will not receive this return connection and cannot discover and control the exploited machine.[14]

3.3 Creating Demilitarized Zones

Network segmentation has traditionally been accomplished by using multiple routers. Firewalls should be used to create DMZs to protect the control network. Multiple DMZs could be created for separate functionalities and access privileges such as peer connections, the data historian, the Inter Control Center Communications Protocol (ICCP) server in Supervisory Control and Data Acquisition (SCADA) systems, the security servers, replicated servers, and development servers. Figure 9 shows a robust architecture with multiple DMZ deployments.

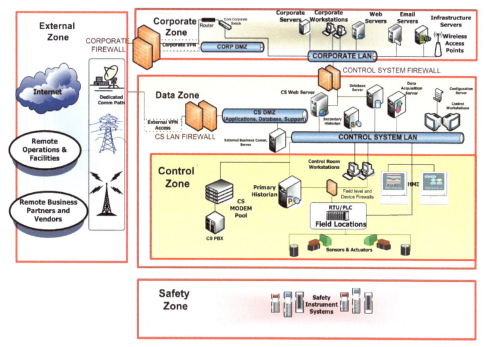

Figure 9. Architecture with DMZ deployments.

All connections to the industrial control systems LAN should be routed through the firewall, with no connections circumventing it. Network administrators need to keep an accurate network diagram of their industrial control systems LAN and its connections to other protected subnets, DMZs, the corporate network, and the outside.

Multiple DMZs have proved to be very effective in protecting large architectures composed of networks with different operational mandates. A perfect example, illustrated in Figure 9, is the conjoined networks for industrial control systems and business. In this example, the secure flow of data into and out of the different environments is critical to operations. Having multiple DMZs protects the information resources from attacks using Virtual-LAN hopping and trust exploitation, and is a very good way to enhance the security posture and add another layer to the defense-in-depth strategy.

3.4 Intrusion Detection Systems

When considering the most logical route an attacker will take in compromising a control network, it is easy to visualize an attack path that pries deeper and deeper into the architecture. Starting from the external environment, an attacker will move past perimeter devices and ultimately strive for access to both the network and hosts on that network. This access may be via field devices where remote access requirements can introduce vulnerabilities into industrial control system architectures. Once on the target network, the attacker must begin to collect intelligence through reconnaissance, followed by attempts at compromising more and more components. In each of these cases, unusual and unauthorized activity would be present in the network, and this activity can be monitored (and acted upon) to provide another level of defense.

Several common methods exist for monitoring a network for unusual or unauthorized activity, with one of the most effective being Intrusion Detection Systems, or IDS. Intrusion detection is not a single product or a single piece of technology, even though commercial "systems" are available. Instead, intrusion detection is a comprehensive set of tools and processes providing network monitoring that can give an administrator a complete picture of how the network is being used. Implementing a variety of these tools helps to create a defense-in-depth architecture that can be more effective in identifying attacker activities, and using them in a manner that can be preventative (i.e., will take action on unauthorized traffic). Figure 10 shows a defense-in-depth strategy with the intrusion detection system.

An IDS, by its very nature, is passive. In a network deployment, the function of the IDS is to watch and assess the traffic or network activity without impacting that traffic. Historically, IDS are placed at ingress/egress points in the architecture, or at the network connectivity points where critical cyber assets are located. Regarding the "security zone" concept, well-defined rule sets pertaining to permitted traffic and data types can be established, thus creating a monitoring capability that can trigger an unexpected or abnormal traffic. Running as a passive device, which may be a mandatory requirement in systems that require high availability, IDS can compare collected traffic against both customized and predefined rules (signature-based) as well as compare against behavior (heuristics-based). IDS compare collected traffic against these rule sets as well as against a set of known attack "signatures." The IDS will investigate a number of traffic attributes, such as port numbers and data payload, to determine if any nefarious (or abnormal) activity is occurring. Having recognized an attack pattern or any deviation from what has been defined as normal/allowable traffic, the systems will carry out a set of instructions that can include alerting a systems administrator. This can have a significant contribution to managing security zones, as each zone can be monitored using detection signatures unique to that specific information enclave. It also helps expedite incident response and resource management, because extensive logging is also a function of most IDS solutions available today.

Most IDSs are signature based, which is acceptable in modern business environments, because an abundance of signatures is available for many network and host architectures using modern protocols and modern operating platforms. Security vulnerabilities in the contemporary business domain are also common, so fine-tuning IDS for networks and hosts using ubiquitous technologies is easy. Like the issues surrounding the deployment of patches and other security technologies in controls systems, the configuration and deployment of IDS are not straightforward. For example, even though many contemporary IDS signatures files are very robust and can detect a wide range of attacks, the signatures required to monitor for malicious traffic in many control networks are not adequate. When looking at the unique communications protocols used in industrial control systems, such as Modbus, ICCP, E/IP, or DNP3, specific payload and port numbers have traditionally not been a part of the signatures seen in contemporary IDS. In short, modern IDS deployed on an industrial control systems network may be blind to the types of attacks that an industrial control system would experience.

However, the work being done in both the research and vendor communities have made tremendous progress in addressing this issue. Organizations specializing in control systems cybersecurity, in collaboration with vendors and integrators, have created a number of useable signatures that are indeed specific to control systems and can be used to monitor for specific attacks that could be targeting either technology or protocols. Although much of the original output from this research was specific to a small number of vendors and applied to only a few protocols, the rate of new signatures being developed is impressive. Today, the availability of new IDS signatures available that are specific to control systems is impressive, and the methodologies used for creating these signatures have provided a framework that empowers asset owners and operators to create their own signatures that are unique to their control system networks.[15] Organizations can also leverage the deterministic nature of their network, and as such create intrusion alarms that are triggered when a deviation from the normal or expected traffic behavior occurs. In essence, thresholds can be established such that when traffic or behavior occurs that is outside of these thresholds an event is triggered. Once thought to be impractical and time consuming, the ability for an intrusion detection system to "learn" network behavior has matured significantly. This heuristic detection has been proven to be very successful in the industrial control arena, and many security vendors (and even some control system vendors) have developed learning engines that can build specific traffic behavior models. The determinism of the control data can greatly improve the granularity of the signatures, because rogue or malicious behavior from an attacker may require actions that would be well beyond expected behavior levels.

In deploying an IDS solution, entities may be tempted to remove some of the default signatures and response capability. This is based on the belief that regular types of attack traffic would never be present on a control systems network, have no relevance to industrial operations, and the large number of pre-existing rules impedes performance of the IDS. However, analysis must be made to ensure that some useful capability of the IDS, capability that could help defend against unseen threats, is leveraged. Many security vendors, including those specializing in industrial control systems security, have created signatures for the IDS that are deployed in control architectures. It is imperative, when deploying IDS on industrial control system networks, that common rules sets and signatures unique to that domain, including some generic signatures, be used. Developing security signatures and rules in a cooperative relationship with the industrial control systems vendor is very advantageous.

One of the common problems observed in industry is that tools deployed for network monitoring are implemented but improperly updated, monitored, or validated. Assigned individuals should be trained and given the responsibility of monitoring system data logs and keeping the various tool configurations current.

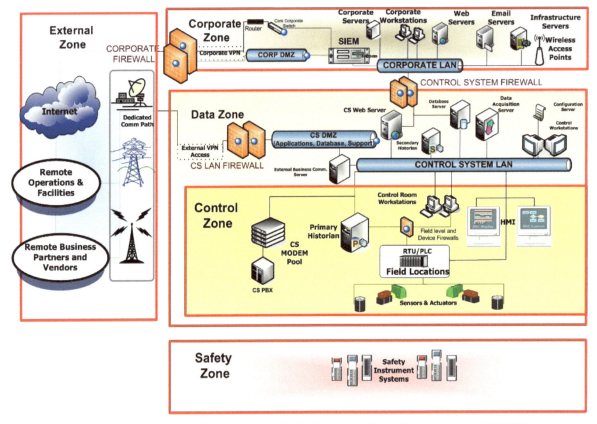

Figure 10. Complete defense-in-depth strategy with the intrusion detection system and SIEM.

Deploying IDS at the host level is similar to deploying it at the network level, but rather than monitoring network activity, the IDS monitors with respect to rule sets. These rules can be very robust and extensive and can include alerting on predefined signatures that are unique to the platform or operating systems that the host is running. IDS placement at the host level provides yet another level of defense-in-depth and can be used to augment the defense strategies deployed at the perimeter and network levels.

Because of the passive nature of IDS, security mitigation and attack realization are a function of how often (and how effective) the analysis of log files is accomplished. Robust policies directing the timely analysis of IDS log is very important. If an attacker is able to gain access to a system and execute an attack prior to the log files being reviewed, IDS and the ability to counter an attack become a moot point. In addition to the commitment an organization must make regarding the collection and analysis of log information, the imperfection of contemporary IDS solutions can create issues regarding "false positives."[h]

3.5   Policies and Procedures

A well-documented and disseminated policy and procedure that is specific to the industrial control systems environment is essential to the success of a defense-in-depth strategy. A yearly review should be completed in recognition of the iterative nature of creating and maintaining policies and procedures.

---

h. A result that is erroneously positive when a situation is normal.

3.5.1   Log and Event Management

As more and more assets are protected with technology, the ability to effectively monitor and support individual security devices diminishes. Modern day security products create large amounts of logs and if monitored separately increase support costs. Security Incident Event Management (SIEM) technologies can be deployed for centralized log and event management. Central consoles give security personnel a complete view of security tools, such as IDS logs, firewall logs, and other logs that can be generated from any number of devices. In some cases, log files can be collected from actual industrial control system elements such as field devices. Figure 10 above shows defense-in-depth strategy with the intrusion detection system and SIEM.

An SIEM product can help streamline incident management and filter out false positives from IDS logs (a process that can be very time consuming). The audit and log files that are aggregated can also be correlated to relate common events to a larger incident. Furthermore, a benefit realized in deploying a SIEM is the extensive visualization capabilities that are offered. Effective visualization of data can help reduce analysis times, improve response capabilities, and simplify the training of new personnel. Sharing and reporting on security data are also added benefits of an SIEM because it can help an organization focus on maintaining its cybersecurity posture. When organizations are able share security data, often in real-time, a common cognitive view of an organization's current security issues matures. This benefit can greatly enhance security communication at all levels of the organization. With accurate and effective communication, residual benefits can be greater security trending, better after-incident reporting, and a clearer picture of the day-to-day operational security readiness.

3.5.2   Security Policy

Effective security policies and procedures are the first step to a secure industrial control systems network. Many of the same policies used for IT security for corporate systems can be applied directly to industrial control system networks, with industrial control system-specific requirements. An example has helped shape the efforts for several initiatives, including the North American Electric Reliability Council (NERC) cybersecurity requirements for electric systems,[16] the Roadmap to Secure Control Systems in the Water Sector,[17] and the Roadmap to Secure Control Systems in the Chemical Sector.[18]

To make the security policy effective, it must be practical and enforceable, and it must be possible to comply with the policy. The policy must not significantly impact productivity, be cost prohibitive, or lack support. This is best accomplished by including both management and system administrator personnel in policy development.

An excellent example of both management and system administrators working together is the development of a control systems "gold disk." A gold disk is a baseline configuration of an operating system that has only the essential ports, services, login credentials, and software needed to effectively run the environment in a safe and efficient manner. Working closely with management and administration to identify the appropriate baseline configuration can greatly increase the security management and lower the attack surface that can potentially be exploited. This can be an effective mitigation against the wide attack surface to which OPC hosts are exposed.[19]

In addition, a gold disk can take advantage of removing all guest and unnecessary user accounts on a system and enforcing that the system be run with individual IDs that have the least amount of privileges that are needed in order to properly operate the system. In doing so, the system can only be modified or changed if an account with the appropriate escalated privileges has been entered. This can significantly reduce the amount of improper use on an industrial control system and can make it much more difficult to install unwanted malicious code on a system.

Another example of a specific policy for industrial control systems is to identify and maintain a procedure for modem security. A good modem policy and procedure lists all modem connectivity, states its purpose, and enforces a centralized list of modem phone numbers. Strong authentication should be in place for modem security with complex passwords in use that are routinely changed in a verified timeframe that management approves.

The procedure should define keeping the modem off and only turning it on manually when needed. If auto-answer functionality exists, the use of the feature should be removed or disabled.

If auto-answer is absolutely necessary, a written justification should be provided to management for a well-documented understanding of the need. For all modems enabled with auto-answer, the procedure should require automatically disconnects with an immediate call back number that is preprogrammed into the modem's memory for reconnections. This technique is an excellent defensive measure when the modem has only one particular line back to which it can communicate. An excellent resource for modem security is the DHS *Recommended Practice for Securing Control System Modems*.6

Security policy can be very effective for wireless communication as well. A wireless security policy for planning, deploying, and configuring wireless access points can be an effective countermeasure from illicit access such as Wardriving. The wireless security policy should examine all aspects of wireless points such as 802.11, 802.15 (i.e., Zigbee, Wireless HART), radio, and microwave. Countermeasures for wireless should be layered and support a defense-in-depth philosophy and the same concepts that secure physical wired networks should be used for wireless. The wireless security policy should consider and document policies for (1) wireless network segmentation and separation from the wired network, (2) strong authentication and authorization techniques, and (3) traffic filtering based on addresses and protocols.[20] Although it should not be relied on solely, generally, the best security policy for wireless is the enforcement of using only the strongest encryption techniques such as WPA2-AES for 802.11.

Network and industrial control system administrators have technical knowledge, but they also need authorization and support from management to implement the policy. Management must support the appointment and development of appropriate personnel resources to implement and administer industrial control systems security.

3.5.3 Patch Management Planning and Procedures

A good patch management plan and procedure is a necessity within an industrial control systems environment to help create a layer of defense against published vulnerabilities. The fundamentals of a patch management plan start with understanding the vulnerabilities that exist on each particular system. Vulnerability analysis and identification help keep an administrator of an industrial control system aware of each particular device that needs to be updated.

In order to properly deploy a patch to a system, an industrial control systems administrator should ensure that proper backup and recovery plans are in place for each device that exists in the environment. Configuration management, documentation, and an updated archive of the current production code are necessary to ensure the system can be returned to a proper state if the patch affects the system. The patch should be tested in a test bed or a simulation environment that closely replicates the current operational environment. Many vendors have patch management plans that industrial control system administrators can use to verify that individual patches do not impact other areas of the environment.

Administrators should work closely with their vendor to verify their own test results with the approved vendor patch level. This will ensure a double verification process that can increase the efficiency and reliability of the deployment of patches to a vulnerable system. A patch management recommended practice has been published for industrial control systems by DHS and should be consulted to gain a clearer picture on the patch process and creating a patch plan.[21]

3.5.4 Security Training

In many cases, the individuals administering an industrial control systems network may not have adequate security training. This situation is generally because of a lack of funding or appreciation for the importance of this training. Training is a core component of an overarching security awareness program and is composed of several key attributes used to support the protection of key information and information resources.

Security training and robust security awareness programs that are specific to the controls systems domain are critical to the security of the industrial control systems as well as the safety of those involved with any automated processes. Like the security awareness programs that are developed for the corporate domains, the programs that will support industrial control system domains have key components that can help drive a continuous and measurable security posture. Within common security awareness programs, such as those listed in NIST SP800-50, *Building an Information Technology Security Awareness and Training Program,*[22] organizations can create applicable security awareness and training curricula that can include:

- Purpose and scope

- Materials development

- Implementation strategies

- Monitoring and feedback

- Success measurement.

Network security administrators require continuous training to keep up to date with the fast-paced changes and advances in the network security field. This includes the latest network architecture designs, firewall, and IDS configurations. New techniques are developed constantly to attack and to defend computer networks. Comprehensive computer security training is important, not only for system administrators, but also for each user.

Formal training can often be cost prohibitive, but good information can be gleaned from books, papers, and websites on cyber and industrial control systems security. As a specific example, and as an excellent resource for industrial control systems-specific training curricula, the DHS's Control Systems Security Program (CSSP) manages and operates the Industrial Control Systems Cyber Emergency Response Team (ICS-CERT) in coordination with the US-CERT and provides focused operational capabilities for defense of control system environments against emerging cyber threats.[i]

Security training programs should provide annual training that covers all personnel roles and responsibilities. Examples are:

1. Executive level training and awareness

2. Operational level training and awareness

3. Technical level training and awareness of personnel with access to critical cyber assets.

3.5.5   Incident Response and Forensics

To fully support a defense-in-depth strategy, a robust incident response capability is required. In the event a security-related incident occurs in the control systems domain, activities to recognize, respond, mitigate, and resume need to be established.

An incident response procedure will instruct employees on the steps to take if a computer on the network has been compromised. All employees should be trained on, and have access to, the procedure

---

i. CSSP and ICS-CERT encourage you to report suspicious cyber activity, incidents, and vulnerabilities affecting critical infrastructure control systems. Online reporting forms are available at https://forms.us-cert.gov/report/. You can also submit reports via one of the following methods: ICS-CERT Watch Floor: 1-877-776-7585, ICS related cyber activity: ics-cert@dhs.gov General cyber activity: soc@us-cert.gov, Phone: 1-888-282-0870

before an incident occurs. Examples of questions to be answered in the incident response procedure include:

- What are the indications that an incident has occurred or is currently in progress?

- What immediate actions should be taken (e.g., should the computer be unplugged from the network)?

- Who should be notified and in what order? Should law enforcement be consulted?

- How should forensic evidence be preserved (e.g., should the computer be left on to preserve the evidence in memory)?

- How can the affected computers be restored?

Planning for forensic-based evidence gathering in order to have clear proof and understanding as to who, what, when, and where has caused a particular incident can be difficult without proper planning. Forensic plans need to be in place prior to an incident in order to maximize the amount of useable evidence. A robust industrial control systems forensic plan is integrated within the overall incident response plan and understands all the baseline control systems capabilities for forensic evidence within an industrial control systems environment. The forensic plan will need to be a sustainable process that has divided each part of the industrial control systems environment into specific category types based on forensic capabilities. More information on forensics in industrial control systems can be found in the document *Recommended Practice for Creating Cyber Forensics Plans for Control Systems*, available from DHS CSSP. [23]

The National Institute of Standards and Technology (NIST) has developed a Computer Security Incident Handling Guide, SP 800-61, which provides guidance to security personnel in developing an incident response procedure.[24] In addition, US-CERT has extensive information and reporting capabilities available for any industrial control systems security incident. This reporting can be completed at http://www.us-cert.gov/control_systems/.

4. RECOMMENDATIONS AND COUNTERMEASURES

When protecting any information infrastructure, good security starts with a proactive security model. This iterative model is composed of several key security strategies that are illustrated in Figure 11.

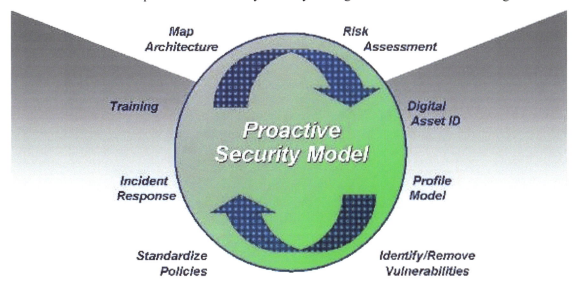

Figure 11. Proactive security model.

Traditionally, development of a defense-in-depth strategy starts with mapping the industrial control systems architecture. Having an accurate and well-documented architecture can enable an organization to be very security-conscious, deploy effective security countermeasures, and be equipped to understand security incidents more readily. Having an understanding of the architecture will allow the administrators to know what they want to protect. A robust understanding of architecture also allows for effective risk assessments, as the development of the assessment parameters and processes can be easily aligned to the existing (and known) information assets in the industrial control systems environment.[25]

Having been able to execute a security assessment, the organization can now assign asset IDs within the control domain, leading to definition of the overall profile of the command and control environment. Following the development of the profile, the defense-in-depth strategy can be deployed. The final phases of the mitigation strategy should involve the deployment of technology that supports recursive and ongoing security training.

4.1 Five Key Security Countermeasures for Industrial Control Systems

Here are five key countermeasures that can be used to drive cybersecurity activities in industrial control system environments.

1. <u>Security policies.</u> Security policies should be developed for the control systems network and its individual components, but they should be reviewed periodically to incorporate the current threat environment, system functionality, and required level of security.

2. <u>Blocking access to resources and services.</u> This technique is generally employed on the network through the use of perimeter devices with access control lists such as firewalls or proxy servers. It can be enabled on the host via host-based firewalls and antivirus software.

3. <u>Detecting malicious activity.</u> Detection activities of malicious activity can be networked or host-based and usually require regular monitoring of log files by experienced administrators. IDS are the

common means of identifying problems on a network, but can be deployed on individual hosts as well. Auditing and event logs should be enabled on individual hosts when possible.

4. Mitigating possible attacks. In many cases, vulnerability may have to be present because removal of the vulnerability may result in an inoperable or inefficient system. Mitigation allows administrators to control access to vulnerability in such a fashion that the vulnerability cannot be exploited. Enabling technical workarounds, establishing filters, or running services and applications with specific configurations can often do this.

5. Fixing core problems. The resolution of core security problems almost always requires updating, upgrading, or patching the software vulnerability or removing the vulnerable application. The software hole can reside in any of the three layers (networking, operating system, or application). When available, the mitigation should be provided by the vendor or developer for administrators to apply.

5. FURTHER READING

- Cyber Risk and Vulnerabilities

  "Mitigations for Security Vulnerabilities Found in Control System Networks"
  http://csrp.inl.gov/Documents/MitigationsForVulnerabilitiesCSNetsISA.pdf, Web site last
  accessed September 2009.

  Common Cyber Security Vulnerabilities Observed in DHS Industrial Control Systems Assessments
  http://www.us-cert.gov/control_systems/pdf/DHS_Common_Vulnerabilities_R1_08-14750_Final_7-
  1-09.pdf, Web site last accessed September 2009.

  "Common Control System Vulnerabilities"
  http://csrp.inl.gov/Documents/05-00993%20r0%20Common%20Vulnerability.pdf, Web site last
  accessed September 2009.

- Security and SQL Attacks

  "Attack Methodology Analysis: SQL Injection Attacks," Abstract
  http://csrp.inl.gov/Documents/SQL%20Abstract.pdf, Web site last accessed September 2009.

- Security and OPC/DCOM

  "Understanding OPC and How it is Deployed"
  http://csrp.inl.gov/Documents/OPC%20Security%20WP1.pdf, Web site last accessed September
  2009.

  Hardening Guidelines for OPC Hosts http://csrp.inl.gov/Documents/OPC%20Security%20WP3.pdf,
  Web site last accessed September 2009.

  "Security Implications of OPC, OLE, DCOM, and RPC in Control Systems," Abstract
  http://csrp.inl.gov/Documents/OPC%20Abstract.pdf, Web site last accessed September 2009.

- Operational Security:

  Using Operational Security (OPSEC) to Support a Cyber Security Culture in Control Systems
  Environments
  http://csrp.inl.gov/Documents/OpSec%20Rec%20Practice.pdf, Web site last accessed September
  2009.

  Creating Cyber Forensics Plans for Control Systems
  http://csrp.inl.gov/Documents/Forensics_RP.pdf, Web site last accessed September 2009.

  Patch Management for Control Systems
  http://csrp.inl.gov/Documents/PatchManagementRecommendedPractice_Final.pdf ,Web site last
  accessed September 2009.

- Modems

  "Securing Control System Modems"
  http://csrp.inl.gov/Documents/SecuringModems.pdf, Web site last accessed September 2009.

- Firewalls

  NISCC Good Practice Guide on Firewall Deployment for SCADA and Process Control Networks
  http://www.cpni.gov.uk/docs/re-20050223-00157.pdf, Web site last accessed September 2009.

  Backdoors and Holes in Network Perimeters: A Case Study for Improving your Control System
  Security
  http://www.us-cert.gov/control_systems/pdf/backdoors_holes0805.pdf

- Wireless

  "Guide for Securing ZigBee Wireless Networks in Process Control System Environments," http://csrp.inl.gov/Documents/Securing%20ZigBee%20Wireless%20Networks%20in%20Process%20Control%20System%20Environments.pdf, Web site last accessed September 2009.

  "Securing Wireless Vlans with 802.11," http://csrp.inl.gov/Documents/Wireless%20802.11i%20Rec%20Practice.pdf, Web site last accessed September 2009.

- Cyber Security Standards

  "A Comparison of Oil and Gas Segment Cyber Security Standards," http://www.us-cert.gov/control_systems/pdf/oil_gas1104.pdf, Web site last accessed September 2009

  "A Comparison of Electrical Sector Cyber Security Standards and Guidelines," http://www.us-cert.gov/control_systems/pdf/electrical_comp1004.pdf, Web site last accessed September 2009.

- NSA Defense-in-depth

  NSA Defense-in-depth http://www.nsa.gov/ia/_files/support/defenseindepth.pdf

- Intruder Detection

  Intruder Detection Checklist http://www.us-cert.gov/reading_room/intruder_det_check.html

- Personnel Security Guidelines

  "Personnel Security Guidelines," http://www.us-cert.gov/control_systems/pdf/personnel_guide0904.pdf

6.   REFERENCES

1. NERC, "Technical Analysis of the August 14th 2003 Blackout," http://www.nerc.com/docs/docs/blackout/NERC_Final_Blackout_Report_07_13_04.pdf, July 13, 2004, Site last accessed October 2009.

2. NIST, NIST SP 800-82 (3-1) has a concise section discussing these differences. "Comparing ICS and IT Systems," http://csrc.nist.gov/publications/drafts/800-82/draft_sp800-82-fpd.pdf, September 2008, Site last accessed October 2009.

3. Troy Nash, "Backdoors and Holes in Network Perimeters," http://www.us-cert.gov/control_systems/pdf/backdoor0503.pdf, August 2005, Site last accessed October 2009.

4. US-CERT, "Security Implications of OPC, OLE, DCOM, and RPC in Control Systems," http://csrp.inl.gov/Documents/OPC%20Abstract.pdf, Site last accessed October 2009.

5. Digital Bond, British Columbia Institute of Technology, and Byres Research,"Understanding OPC and How it is Deployed," http://csrp.inl.gov/documents/OPC%20Security%20WP1.pdf, July 27, 2007, Site last accessed October 2009.

6. DHS, *Recommended Practice for Securing Control System Modems,* http://csrp.inl.gov/Documents/SecuringModems.pdf, January 2008, Site last accessed October 2009.

7. US-CERT, "Attack Methodology Analysis: SQL Injection Attacks," http://www.us-cert.gov/control_systems/csdocuments.html, September 2005, Site last accessed October 2009.

8. DHS, "Common Control System Vulnerability," INNL/EXT-05-00993, Prepared by the Idaho National Laboratory, http://www.us-cert.gov/control_systems/pdf/csvul1105.pdf, Site last accessed October 2009.

9. DHS, *Common Cyber Security Bulnerabilities Observed in DHS Industrial Control Systems Assessements*, http://www.us-cert.gov/control_systems/pdf/DHS_Common_Vulnerabilities_R1_08-14750_Final_7-1-09.pdf, July 2009, Site last accessed October 2009.

10. NSA, "Defense in Depth," http://www.nsa.gov/ia/_files/support/defenseindepth.pdf, Site last accessed October 2009.

11. INL, Using Operational Security (OPSEC) to Support a Cyber Security Culture in Control Systems Environments, Version 1.0," http://csrp.inl.gov/Documents/OpSec%20Rec%20Practice.pdf, February 2007, Site last accessed October 2009.

12. DHS, Department of Homeland Security: Cyber Security Procurement Language for Control Systems, http://www.us-cert.gov/control_systems/pdf/SCADA_Procurement_DHS_Final_to_Issue_08-19-08.pdf, August 2008, Site last accessed October 2009.

13. T. J. Williams Purdue Model for Control Hierarchy ISBN 1-55617-265-6, 1992.

14. NISCC, *NISCC Good Practice Guide on Firewall Deployment for SCADA and Process Control Networks*, http://www.cpni.gov.uk/docs/re-20050223-00157.pdf, February 2005, Site last accessed October 2009.

15. As an example, see http://www.digitalbond.com/wiki/index.php/SCADA_IDS_Signatures, Site last accessed October 2009.

16. NERC, Reliability Standards http://www.nerc.com/page.php?cid=2|20, Date, Site last accessed October 2009.

17. http://www.awwa.org/files/.../PDF/WaterSecurityRoadmap031908.pdf (Unable to locate)

18. DHS, *Roadmap to Secure Control Systems in the Chemical Sector*, http://www.us-cert.gov/control_systems/pdf/ChemSec_Roadmap.pdf, September 2009, Site last accessed October 2009.

19. Digital Bond, British Columbia Institute of Technology, and Byres Research, "Hardening Guidelines for OPC Hosts," For a breakdown of how to create baseline configurations, refer to http://csrp.inl.gov/Documents/OPC%20Security%20WP3.pdf, November 2007, Site last accessed October 2009.

20. Wireless Security for Control systems:

    INL, *Securing WLANs using 802.11i*, Draft, http://csrp.inl.gov/Documents/Wireless%20802.11i%20Rec%20Practice.pdf February 2007, and DHS, *Recommended Practices Guide for Securing ZigBee Wireless Networks in Process Control System Environments*, http://csrp.inl.gov/Documents/Securing%20ZigBee%20Wireless%20Networks%20in%20Process%20Control%20System%20Environments.pdf, April 2007, Both sites last accessed October 2009.

21. DHS, *Recommended Practice for Patch Management of Control Systems*, http://csrp.inl.gov/Documents/PatchManagementRecommendedPractice_Final.pdf, December 2008, Site last accessed October 2009.

22. NIST, "Building an Information Technology Security Awareness and Training Program," http://www.csrc.nist.gov/publications/nistpubs/800-50/NIST-SP800-50.pdf, October 2003, Site last accessed October 2009.

23. DHS, *Recommended Practice: Creating Cyber Forensics Plans for Control Systems*, http://csrp.inl.gov/Documents/Forensics_RP.pdf, August 2008, Site last accessed October 2009.

24. NIST, *Computer Security Incident Handling Guide*, NIST SP 800-61, http://csrc.nist.gov/publications/nistpubs/800-61/sp800-61.pdf, January 2004, Site last accessed October 2009.

25. US-CERT, Regarding self-assessments of controls systems and IT architectures, the reader is encouraged to review the "Cyber Security Evaluation Tool (CSET)," http://www.us-cert.gov/control_systems/satool.html, Site last accessed October 2009.

www.ingramcontent.com/pod-product-compliance
Lightning Source LLC
Chambersburg PA
CBHW042125070326
40689CB00046B/652